I0465703

THE ART OF MANAGING STRESS

Master Your Mind, Build Mental Strength,
Establish Positive Habits, and Achieve Personal
and Professional Growth in Life.

PRADIP DAS

engaging in the rendering of legal, financial, medical or professional advice. The content within this book has been derived from various sources. Please consult a licensed professional before attempting any techniques outlined in this book.

By reading this document, the reader agrees that under no circumstances is the author responsible for any losses, direct or indirect, which are incurred as a result of the use of information contained within this document, including, but not limited to, — errors, omissions, or inaccuracies.

Author Profile

Table of Contents

Table of Contents 4

Introduction 5

Recognizing Your Stressors 11

Developing Healthy Coping Strategies...........20

Time Management Techniques.....................31

Building a Support Network 42

Enhancing Problem-Solving Skills 52

Practicing Gratitude and Positive Thinking 60

Incorporating Relaxation Techniques 71

Nutrition and Lifestyle Changes 83

Finding Work-Life Balance 93

Conclusion..105

Introduction

Stress is something most of us know all too well. It shows up in big moments, like meeting a tight deadline or dealing with unexpected bills, and even in the quieter moments, where it lurks as worry or anxiety. Stress can keep us up at night, make us lose our focus, and leave us feeling drained. But what exactly is this feeling that seems to take over? Why does it have such a powerful hold on us, affecting not only our mood but also our energy, relationships, and even our health?

This book, The Art of Managing Stress, will help you understand what stress is and how it impacts every part of our lives. Think of stress as your body's way of responding to a challenge or demand. Imagine the tension you feel when running late or handling too many things at once. Your heartbeat speeds up, your muscles tighten, and your mind can start to feel overwhelmed. This is your body reacting as if you're in danger—even when you're not. This response is natural, but in our busy world, it can feel like it never switches off. And that's what makes it hard for so many of us to relax.

As we go through this book, we'll explore how stress works and learn ways to take back control over it. We'll look at the physical and emotional sides of stress and understand why it sometimes takes over so quickly. By the end, you'll have new tools to face stressful moments, calm your mind, and keep yourself grounded even when life feels overwhelming.

Stress is a part of life, but struggling under its weight doesn't have to be. As we go through these pages, keep in mind this saying, "Life is 10% what happens to us and 90% how we react to it." With the right understanding and approach, you can turn stress into something you manage, instead of something that manages you.

In understanding stress, it's helpful to consider what causes it. The causes of stress are as varied as the people experiencing it. What might be a mild inconvenience for one person could be overwhelming for another. Some common sources include work pressures, family conflicts, financial worries, health concerns, and time constraints. But stressors don't always come from outside. They can also be internal, like negative self-talk, perfectionism, or high expectations. Some stress can even come from positive experiences like getting married, having a baby, or starting a new job, which add new responsibilities or demands to our lives.

A key to managing stress lies in recognizing the difference between short-term and long-term stress. Short-term stress, also known as acute stress, can actually be helpful. Think of the adrenaline rush you get when giving a presentation or facing a tough decision. It gives you energy, heightens your focus, and pushes you to react quickly. Once the situation is over, your body returns to normal, and you may even feel a sense of accomplishment. But when stress becomes a regular part of life—when it feels like there's always something weighing on you—it shifts from short-term to long-term stress. This chronic stress takes a serious toll on the body and mind, leaving you constantly tense, drained, and often more susceptible to illnesses.

The impact of stress is not limited to a tense feeling in your muscles or the knot in your stomach. Stress has a profound effect on every part of our being. Physically, stress can weaken your immune system, making it harder to fight off infections and even slower to heal from injuries. It can lead to high blood pressure, increased heart rate, and difficulty sleeping, all of which can contribute to more serious health problems over time. Emotionally, stress can lead to feelings of anxiety, irritability, and depression. It often makes it hard to enjoy the things that normally bring joy or to feel motivated in everyday tasks. Mentally, stress can cloud our ability to think clearly, make decisions, and remember details, which can further compound feelings of worry and overwhelm.

What's important to understand is that stress is a part of life. It's not something we can completely avoid, nor should we aim to. But by learning to identify its causes, understanding its effects, and discovering ways to manage it, we can significantly reduce its impact on our lives. This book will guide you through practical, straightforward strategies to help you manage stress in a way that doesn't feel like a chore or a drastic life overhaul.

As we go further, we'll look at real-world tools and approaches that don't require extreme changes but offer meaningful shifts. By recognizing stress early and having a toolkit ready, you can handle life's challenges in a way that keeps stress from taking over. Whether you're dealing with a short-term pressure cooker or the slow burn of ongoing stress, the insights and strategies in these pages are designed to give you control, understanding, and peace of mind.

Recognizing Your Stressors

Stress isn't just about big life events or sudden crises. Often, it's the small, everyday moments and routines that sneak up on us, triggering tension without us even noticing. Recognizing what specifically causes you stress is the first step in managing it effectively. This doesn't have to be complicated or overwhelming; it's simply about paying attention to the moments that leave you feeling tense or irritable.

Think about what makes your shoulders tense or gives you that sinking feeling in your stomach. It could be deadlines at work, feeling rushed in the mornings, or even things like crowded places or too much noise. Maybe it's an upcoming event, like a presentation or social gathering, that makes you feel uneasy. Often, stress triggers are related to situations that feel unpredictable, unfamiliar, or out of our control.

Some people find that their stress is triggered by specific thoughts or worries, like wondering if they're meeting expectations or thinking about the future. Others might feel stress related to their personal relationships or health. Each of us has our own unique set of stress triggers, so your stress won't look exactly like anyone else's. That's why it's so important to figure out what yours are, without comparing them to others.

Start by asking yourself simple questions: What moments in your day feel especially difficult? Are there situations or people that regularly leave you feeling drained? Do certain thoughts or memories make you feel anxious? As you become more aware of your personal stress triggers, you'll be better prepared to handle them. It's not about eliminating all stress (which isn't realistic); it's about recognizing where it comes from.

Keeping a Stress Diary

One of the most practical ways to track your stress is by keeping a "stress diary." Don't worry; this doesn't have to be a huge time commitment. You don't need to write long journal entries, and you don't have to do it every day if that feels overwhelming. Think of it as taking a quick mental snapshot of your stress whenever it pops up, just enough to help you understand it better.

Here's how to get started. When you feel stressed, jot down a few simple details:

1. What was happening? Describe the situation briefly.
2. How did it make you feel? Try to capture the specific emotion, whether it's frustration, anxiety, sadness, or anger.

3. How did you respond? Note anything you did in reaction to the stress, like pacing, getting quiet, feeling like you needed to take a break, or anything else.

You can keep your stress diary in a notebook, on your phone, or wherever you prefer. Some people find it helpful to add extra notes, like how intense the stress felt on a scale of 1 to 10 or whether it affected their ability to focus.

Why does this help? Tracking your stressors over time reveals patterns. For example, you might notice that certain days or times of day are particularly stressful. Or maybe you'll start to see that specific tasks or interactions with certain people bring up more stress than others. These insights can be incredibly useful. When you know your patterns, you can begin to make changes—whether that means adjusting your schedule, finding ways to better prepare for stress-heavy moments, or practicing small steps to stay calm in those situations.

For some, the stress diary process itself can be calming. By putting the feelings down on paper, you're giving yourself a moment to acknowledge the stress instead of letting it build up inside. Over time, you might even start to feel more in control, knowing that you can spot stress as it happens rather than letting it sneak up on you.

Understanding the Stress Response

Once you start noticing your stress triggers and tracking them in your stress diary, it helps to understand what's actually happening inside your body when stress kicks in. This isn't just about knowing the science—it's about understanding why stress feels the way it does and how it impacts both your body and mind.

When you encounter something stressful, whether it's an unexpected phone call, a looming deadline, or even something as simple as being stuck in traffic, your body automatically goes into what's known as the "fight-or-flight" response. This is an ancient response designed to help us survive dangerous situations. Back when humans had to worry about wild animals and natural threats, the fight-or-flight response kept us alert, giving us a quick burst of energy to escape danger.

Most of our stress doesn't come from physical threats. Instead, it comes from thoughts, worries, and everyday pressures. Even so, our bodies respond to these modern stressors in much the same way they would to an actual danger. When you feel stressed, your brain sends signals to your adrenal glands, which then release hormones like adrenaline and cortisol. These hormones cause physical changes: your heart rate speeds up, your muscles tense, your breathing quickens, and your senses become sharper. This can be helpful in some situations, like if you need to react quickly, but over time, repeated stress can start to take a toll.

If you've ever felt your heart pounding before a big presentation or found yourself clenching your fists during a difficult conversation, that's the fight-or-flight response in action. And if you've noticed that these reactions leave you feeling drained or exhausted afterward, it's because your body is burning energy to keep you alert and focused.

While a little stress can be useful, chronic stress—when your body is stuck in this heightened state for long periods—can lead to health issues. It can affect your sleep, digestion, immune system, and even your mental well-being. That's why it's important to recognize and understand your stress response. Once you know what's happening inside your body, you can start to take simple steps to manage it better.

One effective approach is to practice relaxation techniques, like deep breathing, which can help calm the nervous system and bring your body back to a relaxed state. Exercise can also play a huge role, as it allows your body to "burn off" some of the stress hormones, which can make you feel better both physically and mentally.

Recognizing your stressors isn't about adding extra work to your life—it's about simplifying. When you identify the specific triggers and patterns that cause stress, you gain a clear sense of what's affecting your peace of mind. With a simple tool like a stress diary and a basic understanding of how stress affects your body, you're already taking steps to reduce stress. This isn't about getting rid of stress completely (that's impossible for any of us); it's about learning how to respond to it in a way that keeps you feeling steady and in control.

In the next chapters, we'll explore some specific strategies you can use to manage your stress in everyday life. These tips aren't one-size-fits-all; they're designed to give you a range of options so you can find what works best for you. As you keep going, the goal is to build a set of habits and responses that make stress feel more manageable, no matter what life throws your way.

Developing Healthy Coping Strategies

Everyone goes through stress, frustration, or sadness in life. Some days are tougher than others. Finding ways to deal with these feelings in a healthy way isn't just helpful—it's necessary for a balanced, fulfilling life. Learning how to manage stress with positive outlets can improve your mood, health, and overall well-being. This chapter will explore three key areas that can make a big difference in handling difficult emotions: physical activity, creative expression, and mindful practices.

When you build healthy habits in these areas, you'll be better prepared to face whatever life throws your way. Let's take a closer look at the importance of finding positive outlets and how they can help you feel more in control, centered, and strong.

The Importance of Healthy Outlets

When tough times hit, people react in all kinds of ways. Some turn to unhealthy distractions, which may seem to help in the moment but don't actually solve the problem. Unhealthy habits might include overeating, withdrawing from friends and family, or even picking up harmful substances. Over time, these actions can end up making things worse, leading to bigger problems for your physical and mental health.

On the other hand, positive coping strategies are like a safety net—they help you feel better without causing harm. Instead of bottling up feelings, positive outlets provide a release. They allow you to work through challenging emotions instead of avoiding them.

A healthy coping strategy can be something simple, like going for a walk, or more involved, like keeping a journal or painting. What matters is that it helps you manage feelings in a way that leaves you feeling lighter, stronger, and ready to take on what's next. Having a few reliable, healthy outlets on hand can make it easier to handle stress and give you something productive to turn to when you're feeling down or overwhelmed.

Physical Activity as a Stress Reliever

One of the most powerful ways to deal with stress is to move your body. Exercise can be as simple as a brisk walk or as challenging as a workout at the gym. The trick is to find something you enjoy doing. Physical activity not only keeps your body fit, but it also boosts your mood. When you exercise, your brain releases chemicals called endorphins, which act as natural mood lifters. Endorphins help relieve stress and even ease pain. That's why people often feel better—even if they were having a rough day—after being active.

You don't have to be an athlete to benefit from exercise. There are plenty of ways to fit physical activity into your day that don't require special skills or equipment. Dancing, stretching, gardening, or even taking the stairs instead of the elevator can make a difference. And if the idea of exercise feels intimidating, try starting with something you already enjoy. Playing with your pet, riding a bike, or throwing a frisbee in the park can all be great ways to move your body without feeling like you're doing a workout.

Getting outside can also lift your spirits. Fresh air and nature can have a calming effect, reducing stress and helping you feel grounded. If you're in a place where you can go for a walk or sit in a park, take advantage of it. A little sunshine and a break from screens can help you clear your mind.

Physical activity isn't just good for the body it's powerful for the mind, too. Whether you go for a run, join a local sports team, or practice yoga, any movement that gets your heart rate up can be a valuable tool in handling life's ups and downs.

Creative Expressions: Art, Music, and Writing

Another way to handle stress and tough emotions is to let your creativity flow. Art, music, and writing offer ways to express feelings that might be hard to put into words. These activities help you process what you're going through in a unique way and allow you to make something meaningful out of it.

Art

Creating art isn't just for professional artists. You don't need to be skilled to benefit from drawing, painting, or making a collage. Art can be deeply relaxing, and it lets you explore feelings without needing to say a word. For some, the repetitive motions involved in activities like drawing or knitting can feel meditative, making it easier to let go of stress. Experiment with different forms of art, whether it's sketching, coloring, or even sculpting, and see what resonates with you.

If you're unsure where to start, try coloring books or doodling on a piece of paper. These simple activities can be a good way to get started and don't require special tools or techniques. The goal is to focus on the process rather than the end result. When you're absorbed in making art, worries tend to fade, giving your mind a break from stress.

Music

Music has a way of reaching us on a deep level.
Listening to a song that matches your mood can
feel comforting and help you feel understood.
Playing an instrument or singing along to your
favorite tunes allows you to express yourself
without speaking. If you're feeling down,
creating a playlist of uplifting songs can boost
your mood, while soothing music might help if
you're feeling overwhelmed or anxious.

Playing an instrument, even if you're a
beginner, can be a wonderful way to unwind.
Learning a new song or practicing chords gives
your mind something to focus on, helping you
take a break from whatever is causing you
stress. If you're not musically inclined, just
listening to music that makes you feel good can
still have a big impact.

Writing

Writing is another powerful way to work through thoughts and emotions. Some people find it helpful to keep a journal, where they can jot down whatever's on their mind. Writing out your thoughts can help you make sense of them, almost like talking to a friend. Sometimes, things feel less overwhelming when they're on paper.

You might start by writing about your day or listing things you're grateful for. If you're dealing with a specific problem, writing about it can help you look at it from a new perspective. Poems, short stories, or letters you never intend to send can all help in working through emotions. Writing has no rules, so let your pen flow with whatever comes to mind.

Whether it's art, music, or writing, creative expression can be a safe and fulfilling way to manage feelings and reduce stress. These activities are also incredibly flexible; you can do them anywhere, anytime, and adapt them to suit your mood and needs.

Mindful Practices and Finding Balance

Alongside physical activity and creative outlets, mindful practices offer another way to stay calm and steady. Practices like deep breathing, meditation, or just being present in the moment can keep your mind from getting tangled up in worry or stress. These practices remind you to take a pause, to slow down, and to focus on what's right in front of you.

If you're new to mindful practices, start small. Try closing your eyes and taking a few deep breaths whenever you're feeling tense. Imagine the air filling your lungs and then gently letting it out. Even just a minute or two of this can make you feel a little lighter. Apps and online videos can also help guide you through simple meditation exercises if you want to give it a try.

These mindful moments aren't meant to solve problems but to give you a bit of space in your mind, a break from stress, and a chance to reset. Practiced regularly, mindfulness can make a real difference in how you respond to challenges and help you feel more grounded.

Putting It All Together

Healthy coping strategies are a bit like a toolbox. You can pick different tools depending on what you need at the moment. Some days, a good workout might be all you need to feel better. Other days, drawing or journaling might help you sort through more complicated feelings. And sometimes, taking a deep breath and focusing on the present moment can be the quickest way to find calm.

Each strategy can play a role in helping you manage stress, and by having a few options, you can turn to the one that feels right for you. There's no one-size-fits-all solution, and that's the beauty of it—you get to figure out what helps you most.

Building these positive habits now means you'll always have something helpful to turn to when life feels overwhelming.

Time Management Techniques

Time is one of our most precious resources, yet it often slips through our fingers. Without a plan, even the most motivated among us can feel overwhelmed or out of control. That's why effective time management is so powerful. In this chapter, we're diving into techniques to help you organize your time in ways that keep you on track without feeling stressed or overworked. By breaking down tasks, setting clear boundaries, and using methods like the Pomodoro Technique and time blocking, you'll find new ways to handle your workload while keeping your well-being intact.

1. Prioritizing Tasks Effectively

One of the most common time management struggles is knowing what to focus on first. You might have a dozen things on your plate, and it's tempting to tackle them all at once. But, that's rarely the most effective approach. Prioritizing helps you decide where to start and how to work through everything on your list.

The Eisenhower Matrix

A classic method for prioritizing tasks is the Eisenhower Matrix, which divides tasks based on urgency and importance. Picture a box with four sections:

1. Urgent and Important: These tasks demand immediate attention and should be at the top of your list. Examples might be a looming work deadline or a family emergency.

2. Important but Not Urgent: These are your long-term goals, like planning a new project or taking a course to advance your skills. They're important, but you can schedule them without pressure.

3. Urgent but Not Important: These tasks need attention but aren't crucial to your goals. They might be things like replying to non-critical emails or handling quick requests. If possible, delegate them.

4. Neither Urgent nor Important: These are the tasks that can eat up your time without adding value. Aim to limit or eliminate them from your day. This might include browsing social media or checking emails every few minutes.

Using the Eisenhower Matrix to categorize tasks helps you focus on what matters most without getting sidetracked by tasks that don't bring real progress. If you're ever feeling stuck, just check the matrix and work from top to bottom, left to right.

Task Bundling

Sometimes, tasks that seem small can disrupt your focus. Task bundling groups similar activities to handle them in a single block of time. For example, set aside one block for responding to all emails rather than answering each one as it comes in. Similarly, if you have several errands to run, try to do them all in one trip. Bundling lets you stay focused on bigger tasks without getting pulled away for minor ones.

Setting Priorities with the ABCD Method

The ABCD Method is a quick way to assign priorities to tasks by categorizing them as:

- A: Critical – Must be done today.
- B: Important – Should be done today if possible.
- C: Optional – Nice to get done, but not essential today.

- D: Delegate – Hand off to someone else if possible.

The ABCD Method is perfect if you prefer a simple, no-nonsense system. It's an easy way to glance at your list and know where to start.

2. Setting Boundaries and Saying No

A significant part of time management is knowing when to say "no." Many of us feel pressure to say "yes" to every request, from extra work assignments to favors for friends. But, without boundaries, you'll end up stretched thin, exhausted, and unable to give your best to the things that truly matter.

The Art of Saying "No"

Saying "no" doesn't have to be confrontational. It's all about being honest and polite. When someone asks for your time, you don't need to apologize or feel guilty. For example, if a colleague asks you to take on an extra task, a simple, "I'm currently focused on other priorities," is polite but firm.

Establishing Personal Boundaries

Boundaries help you protect your time and energy. Start by identifying where your limits lie. Ask yourself: What am I willing to take on? What am I not?

Once you know your limits, communicate them clearly. For example, if you're working from home and need quiet time in the mornings, let family members know your schedule. Or, if you don't respond to work emails after hours, set an "Out of Office" message during that time.

Boundaries make a huge difference in how you feel and perform. Without them, others may take more of your time, even unintentionally. Setting clear boundaries protects your well-being and ensures you have time for things that matter most to you.

Minimizing Interruptions

Interruptions can derail even the best-laid plans. Simple strategies, like turning off non-essential notifications or finding a quiet workspace, can make a big difference. If you work in an environment where interruptions are common, try a visual signal, like headphones or a "do not disturb" sign, to indicate focused work time.

3. The Pomodoro Technique and Time Blocking

When it comes to staying focused, few techniques are as popular as The Pomodoro Technique and time blocking. Both help you structure your day and maintain momentum.

The Pomodoro Technique

Developed in the 1980s, the Pomodoro Technique is a time management method that encourages working in focused intervals, or "Pomodoros," typically 25 minutes long, followed by a short break. Here's how it works:

1. Set a timer for 25 minutes and focus on one task during that time.
2. When the timer goes off, take a 5-minute break.
3. Repeat this cycle four times, then take a longer break of 15-30 minutes.

The Pomodoro Technique's simplicity makes it effective. Knowing there's a break coming soon helps you stay focused during each interval. Plus, the frequent breaks keep you energized and reduce burnout.

Time Blocking

Time blocking involves setting aside specific chunks of time for different activities throughout your day. Instead of working from a to-do list, you schedule time for each item. This could mean blocking out two hours for writing, an hour for exercise, and thirty minutes for responding to emails. Here's how to get started with time blocking:

1. List your tasks for the day.
2. Estimate the time needed for each task.
3. Assign a time slot for each task in your schedule.

Time blocking provides structure and forces you to be realistic about how much you can accomplish in a day. Unlike the Pomodoro Technique, which is focused on short bursts, time blocking gives each task a dedicated place in your day. If you have a mix of creative work, meetings, and admin tasks, time blocking can be especially helpful.

Using Both Techniques Together

Pomodoro and time blocking can work well together. For example, you might block out a two-hour period for a specific project, but work on it in Pomodoro intervals. This combination provides both structure and frequent breaks, keeping your focus sharp and your energy levels up.

Dealing with Overflow Tasks

Despite your best planning, there are days when tasks spill over into other time slots. When this happens, prioritize again to see if the tasks are urgent or if they can be rescheduled. If a task is consistently overflowing, it might need a larger time block, or it may be better suited for another part of your day. Adjusting your time blocks allows you to stay flexible while keeping overall structure in place.

Putting It All Together

Managing time effectively doesn't have to be complicated. It's about finding a balance that works for you and sticking with methods that support your needs and goals. Start with prioritizing, and then look at how you can implement boundaries, Pomodoro sessions, or time blocks to improve your workflow.

With practice, these techniques become second nature, making it easier to tackle your to-do list, avoid burnout, and achieve more without feeling rushed.

Building a Support Network

Building a strong support network is like setting up a solid foundation for handling life's challenges. When stress hits, having people around you who care, listen, and help can make all the difference. This chapter will explore the value of relationships in managing stress, simple steps to build connections with others, and how to communicate what you need to feel supported.

The Role of Relationships in Stress Management

Imagine this: You're dealing with a tough week, deadlines are piling up, and everything feels a bit too much. Now, imagine having a friend you can talk to or a family member who checks in just to see how you're doing. That's the power of a support network. Having people around who care and understand can make stressful situations feel more manageable.

Research has shown that when people have a reliable support network, they often feel less overwhelmed by stress. They don't have to carry every burden alone. Friends, family, and even coworkers can help us see problems from a new angle, offer advice, and sometimes even share the load. A quick conversation or a laugh with someone who gets it can help lift the weight, if only for a little while. Plus, simply knowing that someone is there if you need them can be comforting and reduce feelings of isolation.

It's not just about having people around—it's about having the *right* people. Positive, supportive relationships encourage and energize us, while negative relationships can make stress worse. Building a network of friends and family who genuinely care helps us not only in the tough times but can also boost our overall sense of happiness. So, let's talk about how to start building these connections and bringing supportive people into our lives.

How to Build Supportive Connections

Building strong, healthy relationships doesn't have to be complicated. It starts with small efforts to connect with others. Here are some simple ways to begin building connections with people who can be there for you when times are tough.

1. Start Small and Be Consistent

Begin by reaching out to people you already know, even if it's just with a quick message or a phone call. Consistency is key here—it's not about grand gestures but about showing up regularly. This could mean sending a text every few days to check in, scheduling a monthly coffee with a friend, or calling a family member once a week. These small efforts add up over time and show others that you care about keeping the relationship alive.

2. Make Time for Face-to-Face Interactions

With so much happening online, we sometimes forget how important face-to-face interactions are. Meeting in person (or even on a video call if you're far away) allows you to connect on a deeper level. This is especially important for building trust, as it's easier to show empathy and understanding in person. Make time for these face-to-face moments—they can strengthen relationships much more than only digital conversations.

3. Be Open and Honest

Building a support network involves a certain level of openness. Share a bit about what's going on in your life, both the good and the challenging parts. When people know more about what you're facing, they're more likely to offer the support you need. Being open also encourages others to share their experiences, creating a mutual sense of understanding.

4. Show Appreciation and Offer Help

Strong relationships are a two-way street. Let people know when they've been there for you. Expressing appreciation for someone's time or advice shows that you value their role in your life. Likewise, make an effort to support them when they need it, whether that's lending an ear, helping out, or even offering a small favor. When people feel appreciated and supported, they're more likely to be there for you in return.

5. Get Involved in Activities or Groups

Sometimes, building a support network requires going beyond your immediate circle. Join a local group, club, or class where you can meet people with similar interests. This could be anything from a sports team to a book club or even a hobby group. Shared activities give you a chance to bond naturally with others, making it easier to build genuine connections over time.

6. Don't Rush—Let Things Develop Naturally

Building a strong support network doesn't happen overnight. It takes time for relationships to grow. Avoid pushing or forcing connections. Instead, focus on small, positive interactions, and allow time for trust and closeness to develop. With patience, you'll find that these relationships will become a reliable source of support.

Communicating Your Needs

It's one thing to have a support network; it's another to make sure they know how to support you. Many of us hesitate to tell others what we need, whether out of fear of being a burden or simply not knowing how to bring it up. However, clear communication is key to building a network that truly helps when times are tough. Here are some steps to help you express what you need in a way that feels natural and comfortable.

1. Be Clear and Direct

When you're feeling overwhelmed or need help, let others know specifically what would be helpful. Instead of saying, "I'm stressed," try to be a bit more specific, like "I could really use someone to talk this over with," or "It would help if we could take a break together." People aren't mind readers, so the more specific you are, the more likely they can offer the right kind of support.

2. Choose the Right Time

Sometimes, timing matters. Try to choose a calm moment to bring up your needs instead of waiting until you're overwhelmed or frustrated.

Bringing up your needs in a relaxed setting allows the other person to focus on what you're saying without the distraction of immediate stress. This can lead to a more supportive and positive conversation.

3. Use "I" Statements

When you talk about what you need, focus on using "I" statements. For example, say "I feel better when I can talk things out," rather than "You never listen to me." This makes it clear that you're sharing how you feel, not blaming the other person, which can make them more open to helping you.

4. Don't Apologize for Asking

Asking for support is not a weakness. Everyone needs help sometimes, and it's a normal part of relationships. Avoid apologizing for expressing your needs, as this can make the other person feel uncomfortable or dismiss the importance of what you're asking. Trust that your friends and family want to be there for you just as you would for them.

5. Set Boundaries When Necessary

Supportive relationships don't mean you have to say "yes" to everything. Sometimes, saying "no" or setting a boundary can actually strengthen a relationship by showing mutual respect. Be clear about your own limits. For instance, if you need some alone time, express it politely and let others know you're not rejecting them but just taking time to recharge.

The Benefits of Building Your Support Network

Building and maintaining a support network can help reduce stress, boost resilience, and improve your general well-being. When life throws curveballs, knowing that you have people who care about you can make those challenges feel a little lighter. By taking steps to build positive connections and communicate openly, you're investing in a support network that can stand by you during tough times.

In the end, a strong support network is about more than just managing stress—it's about creating a community of people who celebrate your successes, understand your struggles, and provide a sense of belonging. So, start small, reach out, and build connections that last. Through these simple, consistent actions, you can create a network of support that becomes one of the most reliable resources in your life.

Enhancing Problem-Solving Skills

In life, challenges are like road signs—sometimes they signal something we need to stop and solve, sometimes they show us a new direction. Problem-solving skills can be one of our greatest tools, helping us navigate these tricky turns with confidence and calm. Whether it's a tough decision, a complicated project, or a personal goal we're struggling to reach, having strong problem-solving skills can make all the difference. Here's a straightforward look at ways to make tackling challenges easier, so you can handle whatever comes your way.

Approaching Challenges with a Positive Mindset

First things first, let's talk about mindset. It's easy to feel frustrated or even defeated when we're up against a tough situation, but how we look at problems has a huge impact on how we handle them. Approaching a challenge with a positive mindset is a bit like cleaning a foggy window—it helps us see clearly and makes solutions feel closer than they might seem. When we believe we can solve a problem, we're more likely to keep trying, even when things don't work out right away.

For instance, imagine you're learning to ride a bike. If you start by thinking, "This is going to be hard, I might fall, and maybe I'm just not good at it," you'll probably feel tense and might even avoid trying. But if you think, "I'm going to give this my best shot, and if I fall, I'll get up and try again," you're likely to have a smoother and faster learning experience. Simply believing you can find a way through a problem makes you more likely to succeed because you're already halfway there.

One way to keep this mindset is by asking yourself, "What can I learn from this?" or "How could I make this easier?" These questions turn your focus from feeling stuck to finding a way forward. And every step forward, no matter how small, builds confidence and brings you closer to a solution. So next time you face a tough challenge, try to picture it as a learning opportunity instead of a barrier. This shift can make even the hardest problems feel a bit lighter.

Breaking Down Problems into Manageable Steps

When we look at a big problem all at once, it can feel overwhelming—like staring up at a huge mountain. But if you break that mountain down into small steps, it starts to look less intimidating. Instead of climbing the whole thing at once, you just need to focus on one step at a time. The same idea works for problem-solving. By taking big challenges and breaking them into smaller, manageable parts, you make it easier to keep moving forward.

For example, imagine you're assigned a big project at work. Looking at everything you need to do at once—researching, planning, writing, editing, and presenting—can be overwhelming. But if you divide these tasks into steps, starting with research, then moving on to planning, it suddenly seems more doable. Each part you complete builds your confidence for the next one.

A great technique for breaking down problems is to ask yourself, "What is the first step I can take?" Maybe it's gathering information, setting a timeline, or brainstorming ideas. Once you've done that, you can ask, "What's the next small step?" Little by little, these steps add up, and before you know it, you're well on your way to solving the problem.

Breaking problems into steps also helps you feel progress. Even if you haven't finished the whole project, completing a small part of it gives you a sense of accomplishment and keeps you motivated. You can celebrate each small win, and that momentum will carry you through to the finish line. So, the next time a big problem comes your way, don't tackle it all at once—take it one step at a time.

Learning from Failures

Finally, let's talk about failure. Even the best plans don't always go as expected, and sometimes things just don't work out. It's normal to feel disappointed, but instead of letting failure stop us, we can use it to improve. Think of failure as feedback; it's a chance to understand what didn't work and why, so we can make a better plan next time.

Imagine you're learning to cook a new dish, but it doesn't turn out the way you hoped. You could give up and decide you're just not good at cooking, or you could take a closer look at what happened. Maybe the oven temperature was too high, or maybe the ingredients weren't quite right. Figuring out what went wrong gives you a better shot at getting it right next time. Each mistake brings a bit more knowledge and gets you closer to success.

One helpful habit is to ask yourself after any setback, "What did I learn from this?" or "What would I do differently next time?" These questions make failures feel less like dead ends and more like stepping stones. Over time, these lessons pile up, and you'll find yourself handling new challenges with more skill and confidence because of the things you've learned along the way.

It's also important to remember that everyone fails sometimes. If you talk to anyone you admire—whether it's a friend, a family member, or a famous person—they'll likely tell you about times they stumbled, too. Failure is part of growth, and it's often the most successful people who have learned to bounce back from it the best. When you stop seeing failure as something negative and start seeing it as part of your learning journey, you'll feel stronger and more prepared to take on whatever comes next.

Putting It All Together

Improving your problem-solving skills isn't something that happens overnight. It's a gradual process that gets better with each challenge you tackle. By approaching challenges with a positive mindset, breaking them down into small steps, and learning from any mistakes along the way, you're building a foundation of resilience and confidence. These skills don't just help with specific problems; they make you feel more capable in all areas of life.

The next time you face a tough problem, try to remember these steps. Start with a positive attitude, focus on what you can learn, and take things one small step at a time. You'll likely find that even the biggest challenges aren't as overwhelming as they first seemed. With practice, problem-solving becomes less about finding the "right" answer and more about discovering the best path forward for you. So keep trying, keep learning, and keep moving forward—you're developing skills that will serve you well for a lifetime.

Practicing Gratitude and Positive Thinking

Gratitude might sound like just a polite "thank you," but it's so much more. When we make a habit of being grateful, it can actually change the way we handle stress. Imagine having a superpower that helps you calm down in tough moments or bounce back when life throws challenges your way. Gratitude is like that—it can shift how we see our world, especially when things are hard.

Stress has a sneaky way of taking over our thoughts, making every problem seem bigger than it actually is. We worry, feel frustrated, or get anxious. But gratitude changes our perspective. By focusing on the good things in our lives—even the small ones—we're not ignoring our challenges. Instead, we're giving ourselves a mental break, a chance to see that there's more to life than our worries. This shift has real effects on our well-being, even affecting our bodies, helping us feel less tense, and promoting a sense of calm.

How Gratitude Works in Real Life

Practicing gratitude isn't complicated. It's about noticing things you might normally overlook. Did someone hold the door for you today? Did you have a moment to sit down and enjoy your favorite drink? Did you share a laugh with a friend? These moments might seem small, but they can make a big difference in how we feel day to day.

Imagine you're having a bad day, filled with stress and disappointment. Instead of letting those feelings pile up, try looking for one thing that went right, no matter how tiny. This act of looking for the good can feel like opening a window in a stuffy room, letting in fresh air. The more we focus on these small positives, the better we become at seeing them all around us. And over time, this habit helps reduce our overall stress levels.

Simple Gratitude Exercises

If you're new to practicing gratitude, don't worry—there's no right or wrong way to do it. Here are some easy ways to get started:

1. Gratitude Journaling: Take a few minutes each day to write down things you're thankful for. Start with three. They can be big or small. Over time, you might start noticing more good things around you.

2. Say Thank You: Show appreciation to people in your life, even for little things. Thank your family, friends, coworkers, or even a stranger. Sometimes, just

saying "thank you" can boost your mood.

3. Mindful Moments: Pause for a moment during your day to appreciate what's around you. Notice the weather, a song you like, or the taste of your food. Being present can help you find joy in simple things.

4. Reflect on Challenges: Sometimes, gratitude can come from hard experiences. Think back to something that was difficult but taught you a lesson. This can help you see growth in challenging times.

Gratitude isn't about pretending everything is perfect; it's about finding something positive, even in tough moments. When we see our lives with a bit more gratitude, our stress has less room to grow.

Techniques for a Positive Mindset

A positive mindset doesn't mean ignoring the tough stuff; it's about choosing to look at things in a way that doesn't let problems weigh us down. People with a positive outlook aren't constantly happy or untouched by stress—they just don't let challenges define their days. Adopting this mindset helps us face obstacles with more energy, and it keeps our mood from sinking when things don't go as planned.

So, how can we build a more positive outlook? Start with small steps and easy techniques. Positive thinking is like building any habit: it takes a bit of practice. But once you get the hang of it, it can make a world of difference in how you feel.

Practical Ways to Think Positively

1. Focus on Solutions: When you face a problem, try to think about solutions

instead of dwelling on the issue. For example, if you're stuck in traffic, focus on how you can make the best of it, like listening to your favorite music or catching up on a podcast.

2. Celebrate Small Wins: Did you finish a task you've been putting off? Did you have a productive meeting or a good workout? Take a moment to appreciate these little victories. Each small win adds up, helping you feel more capable and positive.

3. Avoid Comparisons: It's easy to fall into the habit of comparing ourselves to others, but this rarely leads to happiness. Instead, focus on your own progress. Try to be better than you were yesterday, not better than someone else.

4. Look for the Silver Lining: When something goes wrong, try to find one

small good thing in the situation. Maybe you're stuck at home on a rainy day, but you finally have time to read that book or watch that show you've been meaning to catch up on.

5. Surround Yourself with Positivity: Spend time with people who lift you up and make you feel good. If you're around people who are positive and supportive, their attitude can rub off on you.

Practice Self-Compassion

A positive mindset also involves being kind to yourself. We're all going to make mistakes, and that's okay. Instead of beating yourself up when things don't go as planned, treat yourself like you would a friend. Say to yourself, "It's okay, I did my best," or "I'll try again tomorrow." Being kind to ourselves can help us stay motivated and make it easier to keep a positive outlook.

Reframing Negative Thoughts

We all have negative thoughts from time to time; it's just part of being human. But if these thoughts become a regular pattern, they can shape our mood, actions, and even how we see ourselves. Reframing these thoughts is a way to take back control, allowing us to look at situations more realistically and with less negativity.

Reframing doesn't mean pretending that everything is great; it's about challenging thoughts that might be too harsh or unfair. Imagine you make a small mistake at work and instantly think, "I'm so bad at this." Instead of letting that thought take over, you can reframe it. Ask yourself, "Is that really true?" or "What can I learn from this?" This way, the thought shifts from being discouraging to being useful.

Steps to Reframe Negative Thoughts

1. Notice Negative Thoughts: The first step is awareness. Try to notice when you're being hard on yourself or seeing things in a "worst-case scenario" way. The quicker you catch these thoughts, the easier it becomes to change them.

2. Challenge Your Thoughts: Ask yourself if the thought is accurate or if it's an exaggeration. Sometimes, our minds make situations seem worse than they are. For example, if you're worried about an upcoming presentation, instead of thinking, "I'm going to mess this up," you could think, "I've practiced, and I'll do my best."

3. Replace with a Balanced Thought: Instead of letting the negative thought stick, replace it with a more realistic one. For example, if you think, "I can't do this," try changing it to, "This is hard, but I can ask for help if I need it."

Balanced thoughts are not overly positive; they're just more realistic.

4. Focus on What You Can Control: Negative thoughts often focus on things we can't change. Instead, focus on what you can do right now. If you're nervous about a conversation, focus on preparing what you want to say rather than worrying about how the other person will react.

Building a Habit of Reframing

Reframing is a skill, and like any skill, it takes practice. Over time, it becomes easier to catch negative thoughts and look at situations from a new angle. You may even start to notice that your first reaction to challenges becomes less negative.

Final Thoughts

Practicing gratitude, positive thinking, and reframing negative thoughts are small changes, but they can have a big impact. They don't require extra time or complicated steps—just a bit of attention and an open mind. Life is always going to have ups and downs, but with these tools, you'll feel better equipped to handle them. Instead of letting stress and negativity take the lead, these habits help you stay grounded, balanced, and even a little happier each day.

Incorporating Relaxation Techniques

Stress has a way of sneaking up on us. It builds up quietly, often without us even realizing it, and before long, we feel its weight on our shoulders, tight in our muscles, and even in our minds. So, learning some basic, easy-to-do relaxation techniques can make a big difference in feeling better overall and managing stress before it becomes overwhelming.

In this chapter, we'll explore a few simple ways to relax that you can fit into your daily life. These aren't about major lifestyle changes— they're small practices that can take just a few minutes but help shift your mind and body into a state of calm. We'll cover breathing exercises, progressive muscle relaxation, visualization techniques, and the value of being in nature.

Let's dive in and see how these can work for you.

Breathing Exercises and Progressive Muscle Relaxation

When life feels chaotic, our bodies and minds often reflect that tension. You might notice your shoulders creeping up toward your ears, or find yourself clenching your jaw. It's common, but there are easy ways to help your body let go of these stress signals. Breathing exercises and progressive muscle relaxation are simple, effective ways to release physical tension.

Breathing Exercises

Our breath is with us all the time, but it's amazing how often we forget about it. When we're stressed, our breathing tends to get faster and shallower, which can make us feel even more on edge. Deep breathing exercises are an easy way to calm things down and help you feel more in control.

1. Simple Deep Breathing: Find a comfortable spot—sitting, standing, or lying down—and take a deep breath in through your nose, feeling your belly rise as you fill your lungs with air. Hold it for a moment, then let it out slowly through your mouth. Repeat this a few times. As you breathe, try to focus only on the air coming in and going out, letting go of any thoughts or distractions.

2. Box Breathing: This technique involves a simple pattern—inhale for four seconds, hold for four seconds, exhale for four seconds, and pause for four seconds before starting again. Picture a box, moving from one corner to the next with each step. It's easy to remember and gives your mind a gentle

focus, which can help quiet those racing thoughts.

3. 4-7-8 Breathing: For this one, breathe in through your nose for a count of four, hold for seven, and then exhale completely through your mouth for a count of eight. This type of breathing slows the heart rate, which can help create a natural feeling of calm.

These exercises are quick to do and can be done anywhere—at your desk, in bed, or even while waiting in line. Just a few minutes of focused breathing can help calm nerves, refocus the mind, and reduce tension.

Progressive Muscle Relaxation (PMR)

Progressive Muscle Relaxation is a way to bring awareness to areas in your body that may be tense, helping you release that tension bit by bit. It involves tensing and then relaxing each muscle group, starting from your toes and working up to your head.

Here's a step-by-step guide to try PMR:

1. Get Comfortable: Sit or lie down in a comfortable position where you won't be disturbed.

2. Start with Your Feet: Begin by focusing on your feet. Tense the muscles in your toes and feet as you breathe in, holding for a few seconds. Then, as you breathe out, relax the muscles and feel the tension melt away.

3. Move Upwards: Shift your focus to your calves. Tense, hold, and release. Continue this pattern, working up through your legs, torso, arms, shoulders, and finally your face. You might be surprised at how much tension we unknowingly carry in our jaws or around our eyes.

4. Notice the Difference: After tensing and releasing each area, take a moment to notice how much lighter it feels. By the end, your whole body should feel noticeably more relaxed.

Progressive Muscle Relaxation takes a bit of practice, but it's a great tool for calming both body and mind. And it's especially helpful at night if you're someone who finds it hard to switch off and fall asleep.

Visualization Techniques

Our minds are incredibly powerful, and visualization is a way to use that power to our advantage. Even just imagining a calm, peaceful place can have a real impact on how we feel physically and emotionally. Visualization can help distract from stress and bring a sense of peace and comfort.

Guided Imagery

One popular type of visualization is guided imagery, where you picture a scene that feels safe and relaxing. You don't need any special skills—just your imagination.

1. Choose Your Setting: Think of a place where you feel calm and safe. This might be a beach with waves lapping against the shore, a forest with tall trees around you, or even a cozy room with a soft chair. Try to imagine as many details as you can: What does it smell like? What sounds do you hear? How does the air feel against your skin?

2. Immerse Yourself in the Scene: Let yourself fully enter this setting. If it's a beach, picture the warmth of the sun, the feel of the sand under your feet, and the gentle sound of waves. Take

slow, deep breaths and allow yourself to feel as if you're truly there.

3. Return Slowly: After a few minutes, take a deep breath and gently bring yourself back to your current surroundings. Even a brief visualization session can bring a sense of relief and help you feel more at ease.

Positive Visualizations for Daily Life

Visualization isn't just for imagining calm places; you can also use it to handle upcoming situations with confidence. For instance, if you're anxious about a meeting or a presentation, spend a few moments visualizing yourself going through it calmly and successfully. Imagine yourself speaking clearly, feeling prepared, and receiving positive feedback. This kind of practice can help reduce anxiety and give you a boost of confidence.

Visualization is like a mental break from the pressures around us. With practice, it can become a valuable tool to keep stress levels down and help you manage life's challenges with a little more ease.

Engaging in Nature and Outdoor Activities

Sometimes, the simplest way to relax is just to step outside. Nature has a natural calming effect on us. Research shows that spending time outdoors can help reduce stress, improve mood, and boost overall well-being. You don't need a mountain or a forest nearby to experience these benefits—even a small park, garden, or walk around the neighborhood can help.

Taking a Walk

A short walk outside, even just 10 or 15 minutes, can have a noticeable impact on your mood. Walking lets your mind wander, and if you're surrounded by trees, water, or other natural sights, it can feel even more refreshing. Try to walk at a pace that feels comfortable, letting yourself notice what's around you. The sound of birds, the breeze, or even the feel of sunlight can all help bring a sense of calm.

Connecting with Nature

If you have a bit more time, consider spending a couple of hours in a natural setting. Many people find that activities like hiking, picnicking, or even just sitting in a quiet outdoor spot can create a deep sense of peace. If you live in a city, seek out nearby parks or green spaces. Sometimes, just seeing a bit of greenery can have a positive effect.

Outdoor Activities as a Routine

Creating a habit of spending time outside can be as simple as scheduling a walk a few times a week or visiting a favorite spot regularly. Some people enjoy jogging or biking, while others prefer a more leisurely approach, like gardening or birdwatching. The important part is simply to get out and let nature work its calming magic.

Final Thoughts

Learning to relax doesn't have to be complicated. Sometimes it's as easy as taking a few deep breaths, letting your muscles relax, picturing a peaceful scene, or stepping outside. These small practices can make a big difference in how you feel day to day. And the more you practice them, the easier it gets to tap into these techniques whenever you need them.

Each of these techniques is like a tool in a toolkit. You don't have to use them all at once, and there's no right or wrong way to start. Experiment and find what works best for you, adding these simple moments of calm into your daily routine. With time, you may notice it's easier to manage stress, feel more grounded, and enjoy the little moments that bring peace into your life.

Nutrition and Lifestyle Changes

Good food, good sleep, and a little bit of balance can make a big difference when life gets stressful. In this chapter, we'll look at how what you eat and how you sleep can affect stress levels—and offer some straightforward ways to help you feel more calm and balanced every day. You'll find out why certain foods can calm your nerves, why sleep isn't just a "break" from the day but a reset for your mind, and why the link between diet, sleep, and stress is too important to ignore. Let's get into some practical tips on how a few changes in your daily life can reduce stress in ways you'll actually notice.

The Connection Between Diet and Stress

What you eat has a surprisingly big impact on how you feel. When you're under stress, your body uses more energy and releases chemicals that can take a toll if left unchecked. This can lead to mood swings, exhaustion, and even more stress. A steady diet of nutritious food helps the body handle stress better, while junk food and sugar highs can make things worse.

When stressed, it's easy to reach for comfort foods like sweets, chips, or caffeine-packed drinks. While they might feel good in the moment, they don't help in the long run. Here's why: these foods often cause spikes in your blood sugar, which can lead to "crashes" in energy and mood. The more these highs and lows happen, the more worn out and stressed you might feel.

Instead, foods rich in vitamins, minerals, and proteins help your body stay balanced. They keep your energy steady, improve your mood, and make it easier to handle stress as it comes. Research has shown that certain foods can even directly influence brain function, helping to boost serotonin, the "feel-good" chemical that can help with stress and anxiety.

Foods that Help Manage Stress

If you're wondering which foods are stress-busters, here's a list of everyday options to consider. Each has specific nutrients that support mood and energy without sending you on a blood sugar rollercoaster.

1. Leafy Greens

Spinach, kale, and other greens are packed with folate, which helps produce dopamine, a chemical that makes you feel calm and happy. Research has linked folate to a reduction in feelings of depression and stress. So, adding a handful of leafy greens to your meals can make a positive difference over time.

2. Nuts and Seeds

Almonds, walnuts, chia seeds, and flaxseeds are great sources of omega 3 fatty acids, magnesium, and B vitamins. These nutrients are all important for brain health and can reduce anxiety. Just a handful of these as a snack or mixed into meals can help keep stress at bay.

3. Berries

Blueberries, strawberries, and raspberries are loaded with antioxidants, which can help your body repair itself from stress-related damage. They also have a naturally sweet taste, making them a good alternative to sugary snacks.

4. Avocado

This creamy fruit is rich in healthy fats and potassium, which can help regulate blood pressure, often raised by stress. It's also filling, so it can keep you satisfied and prevent overeating when stressed.

5. Oats and Whole Grains

Oatmeal, brown rice, and quinoa are packed with complex carbs that release energy slowly, helping to stabilize your blood sugar and keep energy levels steady. These foods also encourage serotonin production, which can improve mood and reduce stress.

6. Fatty Fish

Salmon, sardines, and other fatty fish are full of omega-3 fatty acids, which have been shown to reduce inflammation and may help with stress. Omega-3s also support brain health and can reduce the production of stress hormones like cortisol.

7. Dark Chocolate

In moderation, dark chocolate can actually reduce stress! It contains antioxidants that can reduce cortisol levels, which helps with stress. Just a small piece (70% cocoa or higher) can be a satisfying treat without adding too much sugar to your diet.

8. Herbal Teas

Chamomile, peppermint, and green tea are known for their calming properties. Sipping on these teas can be relaxing, and chamomile has been linked to better sleep and reduced anxiety. A warm cup of tea can also be a comforting ritual, especially after a long day.

Eating with a focus on these types of foods won't "cure" stress, but it will help your body handle it better. Think of it as giving your body the tools it needs to cope. You may notice that with these foods in your diet, you feel less overwhelmed, your energy is more consistent, and your mood feels a little lighter.

The Importance of Sleep Hygiene

Good sleep is crucial for managing stress, but stress can make sleep elusive. When you're stressed, you're more likely to toss and turn, find it hard to relax, or wake up during the night. Over time, poor sleep can increase anxiety and make it harder to handle daily stressors, creating a vicious cycle.

Sleep hygiene is all about creating an environment and routine that encourages better sleep. It's not just about getting eight hours—it's about making those hours restful and refreshing. Good sleep hygiene can improve the quality of your sleep, reduce the time it takes to fall asleep, and help you feel more alert during the day.

Here are some practical tips to improve sleep hygiene:

1. Set a Consistent Bedtime and Wake Time

The body's natural clock, or circadian rhythm, works best with regularity. Going to bed and waking up at the same time each day, even on weekends, can make it easier to fall asleep and wake up refreshed. It sets your internal clock and can lead to better quality sleep overall.

2. Limit Screen Time Before Bed

The blue light from phones, tablets, and TVs can interfere with melatonin production, the hormone that signals it's time to sleep. Try to avoid screens at least an hour before bed. Instead, consider reading a book, listening to calming music, or meditating to help you wind down.

3. Create a Relaxing Bedtime Routine

A consistent bedtime routine can help signal to your brain that it's time to wind down. Taking a warm shower, doing gentle stretches, or listening to soothing sounds can relax both your mind and body, making it easier to transition to sleep.

4. Limit Caffeine and Sugar Intake

Caffeine and sugar can stay in your system longer than you might think, especially if consumed in the late afternoon or evening. These stimulants can keep you wired, making it hard to fall asleep or stay asleep.

5. Keep Your Room Dark, Quiet, and Cool

Your sleeping environment can greatly affect how well you sleep. Consider blackout curtains, earplugs, or a white noise machine if outside noise or light bothers you. A cooler room is generally better for sleep, as the body's temperature naturally drops during the night.

6. Avoid Heavy Meals Before Bed

Eating a big meal close to bedtime can interfere with sleep quality. If you're hungry before bed, opt for a light snack that includes a complex carbohydrate and a protein, like a piece of whole-grain toast with almond butter.

Small Changes, Big Benefits

Stress is part of life, but how you eat and sleep can influence how you handle it. The foods you choose and the routines you follow aren't about rigid rules—they're about small choices that add up to make you feel better. By adding nutrient-rich foods and a little sleep routine, you can give your body the support it needs to handle whatever comes your way.

Finding Work-Life Balance

Finding the right balance between work and personal life can feel like trying to juggle while riding a unicycle. Some days, everything falls into place, and others, it feels like all the balls are on the floor. Striking this balance doesn't mean everything has to be perfect every day; it's about small choices that add up to a life you enjoy at work and outside of it.

In this chapter, we'll dive into practical ways to keep your personal and professional lives in sync, using strategies that are simple but effective. You'll see why hobbies are more than just pastimes; they're lifelines to our well-being. And we'll explore tips to create a work environment that feels less like a source of stress and more like a place you can function smoothly. Let's get into it.

Strategies for Balancing Professional and Personal Life

Work-life balance isn't about splitting your day equally between work and relaxation. It's more about managing your energy and focus so you have enough of each for both areas. Here are some straightforward ways to help you set up a realistic balance.

1. Set Boundaries and Stick to Them

One of the easiest ways to stay on top of work and life is to have clear boundaries. If you're working from home, try setting up specific work hours and sticking to them. Turn off email notifications after hours or, if you work in an office, avoid taking work calls during dinner.

Being "off" means truly letting go of work-related tasks, not just physically but mentally too. You can even give yourself a cut-off time each evening when you stop thinking about work tasks or stop worrying about tomorrow's deadlines.

2. Prioritize Tasks Using the "Big Three" Method

Most of us have to-do lists that could stretch around the world. The "Big Three" method can help narrow down your focus. Each morning, pick just three key tasks to complete by the end of the day. These should be tasks that, once done, will make you feel like you had a productive day.

This approach isn't about cutting out all other responsibilities; it's about making progress on the most important items first. You can handle the smaller stuff once these tasks are done. The sense of accomplishment you get from ticking off those top three can give you the motivation to handle anything else that comes your way.

3. Schedule Breaks Throughout Your Day

Many people feel guilty about taking breaks, but taking a few minutes to step away from your desk can actually boost productivity. A simple rule of thumb is the 50/10 rule: work for 50 minutes, then take a 10-minute break.

Short breaks can help refresh your mind and prevent burnout. You might take a quick walk, grab a snack, stretch, or even just stare out the window. The idea is to give your brain a moment to breathe before diving back into work.

4. Learn the Art of Saying "No"

It's hard to say "no" when you're trying to be helpful or want to be seen as dependable, but constantly saying "yes" to every request can stretch you thin. Learning to decline some requests or projects means you can fully commit to the ones that matter most to you.

The trick is to be polite but firm. You could say something like, "I'd love to help, but I'm at my capacity right now." This lets others know you're willing to help when you can, but also sets a respectful boundary.

5. Use Technology to Your Advantage

Technology can be a distraction, but it can also be a great tool for managing time. Many apps help with task management, from to-do lists to calendar reminders. Tools like these can help you streamline work tasks and keep track of your schedule, so you have more control over your day.

But don't go overboard with tech. Choose just one or two apps that fit your needs, and make them part of your daily routine. This way, you'll stay organized without spending all your time managing tools instead of tasks.

The Role of Hobbies and Interests

Having hobbies and interests isn't just about having something to do in your free time; it's about building a fulfilling life outside of work. Whether it's cooking, hiking, painting, or learning a new language, hobbies give you a break from your work mindset, which can improve your mood and reduce stress.

1. How Hobbies Improve Your Mental Health

Hobbies let you dive into something that's fun, challenging, and rewarding. When you're focused on something you enjoy, it's easier to forget the day's stress. Over time, doing activities you love can have a powerful effect on your mental health, reducing anxiety and even helping to ward off depression.

When you're mentally refreshed, it's easier to approach work with a positive attitude. You might find that a half-hour of reading, playing an instrument, or drawing can give you the break you need to return to work more energized.

2. Hobbies Help Build Skills You Didn't Expect

Hobbies can teach you skills that are useful beyond the hobby itself. For instance, playing a sport can help with teamwork, strategy, and focus. Creative hobbies like writing or painting can improve problem-solving skills and out-of-the-box thinking. Even cooking teaches patience and planning, both valuable in any professional setting.

Think of hobbies as a way to expand your strengths without even realizing it. You might surprise yourself with how often you can apply the patience or discipline from a hobby to tasks at work.

3. Social Hobbies Help Build Relationships

If you're part of a book club, sports team, or cooking class, you're automatically building connections with people outside of work. Social hobbies are a great way to meet people who share your interests and to form friendships based on shared experiences rather than job roles.

Having a supportive network outside of work can help balance the challenges of professional life. Plus, it's nice to have friends you can talk to about something other than your job.

4. Set Aside Time for Hobbies Regularly

Setting aside time for hobbies might seem tricky when your calendar is packed, but it's worth it. Even if it's just an hour on a Saturday morning, having this time can act as a mental refresh button.

The trick is to treat it like an appointment. Make it a priority and avoid the temptation to skip it "just this once." Even a small commitment to doing something you enjoy can recharge your mind and help you feel ready to tackle work tasks when the week begins.

Creating a Stress-Free Work Environment

A calm, organized workspace can make a huge difference in your day. If you feel stressed the moment you sit down at your desk, it's going to be harder to get through the day. Here are some simple ways to make your work environment work for you.

1. Organize Your Desk

A clean, organized desk can make it easier to focus. When you know where everything is, you spend less time hunting for things and more time getting work done. Start by keeping only the essentials on your desk and clearing away clutter.

Even if it's a digital space, keep your computer organized. Close tabs you don't need, use folders to manage files, and make sure your desktop isn't overwhelmed with documents. A clear space can make for a clear mind.

2. Add Personal Touches

It might sound small, but a few personal touches, like a photo, a favorite mug, or a small plant, can make your workspace feel more comfortable. When your desk has items that make you feel happy or relaxed, it can remind you to take a deep breath when work gets stressful.

Just avoid going overboard with decorations. Too much can be distracting, but a few well-chosen items can brighten your workspace.

3. Keep a Routine and Take Breaks

Routines can help you feel more in control of your day. Whether you start your day with a coffee or a five-minute review of tasks, having a small, consistent routine can set the tone for your work. It's a way of signaling to your brain that it's time to focus.

Taking breaks during the day can also make a big difference in managing stress. A quick walk, a chat with a coworker, or even just stretching can prevent your mind from feeling overwhelmed. These breaks are often when the best ideas and solutions come to mind because you've given yourself a moment to relax.

4. Reduce Noise and Limit Distractions

If you work in a noisy environment, noise-canceling headphones or calming background music can help you stay focused. If your workplace is prone to interruptions, try setting "focus hours" when you can work without disturbances.

You might even put up a small sign on your desk or send a message to coworkers, politely letting them know you're concentrating for a while. People are usually respectful when they know you're trying to focus.

Finding work-life balance isn't about making drastic changes. It's about small, steady adjustments that help you enjoy your time at work and outside of it. By creating boundaries, making time for hobbies, and shaping a stress-free workspace, you can feel more in control and get the best out of both worlds.

Conclusion

Managing stress is not merely a task to be checked off a list; it is an ongoing process that requires awareness and adaptability. Life presents a myriad of challenges, and each one has the potential to impact our mental and physical well-being. Recognizing that stress will always be a part of our lives allows us to approach it with a mindset that prioritizes our health and happiness. This journey involves understanding that stress management is not about eliminating stress entirely; rather, it's about developing the skills and tools necessary to navigate it effectively.

Throughout our lives, we will encounter various stressors, from personal challenges to professional pressures. Each of these experiences offers an opportunity for growth. By viewing stress management as a continuous journey, we allow ourselves the flexibility to adjust our strategies as needed. This perspective helps us develop resilience, enabling us to face future obstacles with greater confidence.

Creating Your Personalized Stress Management Plan

A key component of effective stress management is the creation of a personalized plan that aligns with your unique needs and lifestyle. This plan should incorporate a variety of strategies tailored to your individual circumstances, preferences, and stress triggers. Start by identifying what causes you stress and recognizing how you typically respond. Understanding these patterns is essential in developing effective coping mechanisms.

Consider incorporating techniques such as mindfulness, exercise, time management, and social support into your plan. Mindfulness practices, like meditation and deep breathing, can help center your thoughts and provide clarity during chaotic moments. Physical activity, whether through structured workouts or casual walks, is another powerful tool that can significantly reduce stress levels while improving overall health.

Time management plays a crucial role in reducing feelings of being overwhelmed. Create a realistic schedule that prioritizes your responsibilities while allowing for breaks and downtime. This balance is vital for maintaining mental clarity and reducing anxiety. Additionally, don't underestimate the importance of social connections. Building and nurturing relationships can offer emotional support, helping you to navigate through difficult times.

Your personalized plan should not be static. Life changes, and so should your approach to stress management. Regularly assess what is working for you and what may need adjustment. Seeking feedback from trusted friends, family, or professionals can also provide valuable insights.

Encouragement for Continued Growth and Resilience

The journey of stress management is one of personal development and resilience. It is essential to approach this journey with a positive mindset, viewing each challenge as a chance to grow. Over time, you will likely discover strengths you didn't know you possessed, and these insights can empower you to handle future stressors more effectively.

Growth in this area often comes with setbacks, and that is entirely normal. Acknowledge that not every strategy will work every time. Some days will be more challenging than others, and that's a part of the human experience. What matters is how you respond to these challenges. Embrace the idea that resilience is built through adversity; each time you face stress, you have the opportunity to strengthen your ability to cope.

Moreover, take the time to celebrate your progress. Acknowledging even small victories can boost your motivation and reinforce your commitment to maintaining your stress management practices. Whether it's completing a stressful project at work, managing a conflict more effectively, or simply feeling more at ease in your daily life, recognize these achievements as markers of your growth.

As you walk this path, remember that you are not alone. So many others are facing similar challenges, and reaching out can be a powerful way to find strength. Share your journey, listen to others, and welcome fresh perspectives that can guide and uplift you.

Managing stress is not a destination but a journey—one that requires patience, understanding, and kindness toward yourself. By crafting a plan that works for you and viewing each challenge as a chance to grow, you can build resilience and nurture a more fulfilling life. Keep moving forward with assurance, knowing that every effort you make is a step toward a healthier, more balanced you.

As you go, hold close this thought: "In every moment of struggle lies the potential for strength." Carry this mindset with you, and may peace and balance always be within your reach.

Join My Community

https://community.askpndas.com/

www.ingramcontent.com/pod-product-compliance
Lightning Source LLC
Chambersburg PA
CBHW070422240526
45472CB00020B/1143